When life events make
you skeptical about living?

SAVIOR
OVER STRAITJACKET

CHRISTOPHER
GRANVILLE

SAVIOR

OVER STRAITJACKET

CHRISTOPHER GRANVILLE

Printed in the United States of America
First Printing 2021
First Edition 2021

Library of Congress Control Number: 2021925797

10 9 8 7 6 5 4 3 2 1

SAVIOR

OVER STRAITJACKET

This book is dedicated to the memories of my loving parents, Stromme Granville, Sr., and Lucille Granville, as well as my son, Jamison Granville.

Table of Contents

Introduction

> **Savior**
>
> Noun: a person who <u>saves</u>, rescues, or delivers: (initial capital letter) a title of God, especially of Christ.
>
> **strait·jack·et**
>
> Noun: A garment made of strong material and designed to bind the arms, as of a violently disoriented person. Anything that severely confines, constricts, or hinders.

G rief is a mind-numbing process that can grip your entire being if you let it. This book was written as a form of therapy for myself initially, but I now want to share this with those who are facing or will face extreme challenges that they might not be able to handle. The process of handling them could possibly drive you insane or inspire you. I believe if you have faith in yourself and God, **everyone can find healing**.

I am amazed at how my life has turned out to be. I envisioned my life to be totally different than it is currently. Time can work in your favor or disrespect you. One thing is for certain; time will always move in one direction- forward. Whether you are ready for it or not, the trials of life will come. Growth, faith, action, and prayer, along with patience, have assisted me in this journey of healing. I don't take words from people or people themselves for granted because they both can be here today and gone tomorrow. Some emotions can last longer than others, and the person or event that caused the emotion might be long gone even if you are still trying to process how it made you feel. Everyone will be faced with challenges at different stages in their lives. If you live long enough, you will face something. I pray that you also live with a sense of urgency to overcome any challenge that may cause you to question your faith or even your existence. Working through some things will take a toll on you that without the right support, it might leave you more broken than ever. Ask for help, take time to heal, appreciate the good moments, and try not to focus on the bad moments.

Even as this book was being written, I was attacked from different, weird directions, from people and things that were barely present in any helpful way. I was challenged in ways that I really had to call on my Savior for not only guidance but for safety. Straitjacket moments are real, and you will be challenged, especially when you are getting closer to your breakthrough. Just pray for all, especially negative people; maybe they believe hating on others will help them elevate. Who knows? There is a saying on the internet somewhere that says, "Pray for everyone even though some are preying on you." If you live and help others win long enough, I believe that statement to be a fact. No matter your generosity, there are always people that don't want you to be great. They'd rather hate than help and want to see you suffer than seek to help you. Remember, hurt people hurt people. Finding a Savior instead of a straitjacket is a real thing, and this book will hopefully help you identify the importance of that.

Be careful of the energy you allow yourself to be around. People, places, words, and other things can help or hurt your physical as well as your mental health. Don't be afraid to walk away from anything or anyone who drains you emotionally. The right energy can help you to heal and provide you with a better path forward. The wrong energy could hurt, harm, and possibly destroy a brighter future for you and your family. I pray that this book will be a reminder that God is real and that no matter what you think your plan is, God's plan for you is the only one that you should live.

I would have never guessed in a million lifetimes that the things I am going to share with you would happen to anyone, let alone my family and me. "They say the Lord works in mysterious ways, and things work on God's time, not yours or mine." I know now from experience that it's so true in a variety of ways. Also, I have written this book as a reminder that I found a Savior over a Straitjacket, and so can you.

Finding value in life shouldn't have to take extreme losses or sacrifices, in my humble opinion. There is value in life by waking up every morning in helping others, whether it is through laughter, inspiring, praying, or just being yourself. There are times that I wonder why God designed my playbook like this. Why would God want anyone to go through these things? What's his plan, and why are these his plans for me?

Frustration sometimes plays a part in my life still because I have gone through storms that left behind daily aftermaths. Even though the events in this book happened in the past, the events are things I still think about to this day. The clean-up process is constant. I parent and interact with people differently now, and not sure if it's because of the painful events or just leveling up. Some of the events I'll be sharing with you have caused me to do some serious soul searching and reassurance on how mentally strong I needed to be. I was at the bottom of the bottom, and I cried every day for like a year straight. I was ready to go to a dark place and stay there forever. At times, I tried to justify that the dark place was best for me, and God wanted me to be in a dark place. I was at a defining moment in my life and didn't have a clue on how I was going to make it out. But as a kid, I remember my mom always saying, God wouldn't bring you this far just to leave you or forsake you. I needed help but not just regular help; I needed professional help. I believed that if I found professional help, I would be able to stay checked in with reality and not check out from it. I felt I was really at that point in my life that if I didn't get help, then I was going to hurt myself badly. I knew that I had to find a Savior instead of a straitjacket. I want to help others do the same with this book. I don't know who will read this, but I hope you find value in life, and no matter your struggle, remember there is always assistance and prayer. If I can find a Savior instead of a straitjacket, then anyone can.

As a man, especially a black man growing up, I was always told to show no emotion. People will try to use your emotions against you. Suck it up, be a man; you're labeled soft if you let anything get to you. Bury those tears; no one cares; they have their own problems. Looking back at those times, the people saying those things weren't qualified to tell me how to think, feel or act. Basically, they were saying to put a wall up and let no one inside because if someone gets inside, they will turn your life upside down. I think that isn't sound advice; people need to speak to a select group of people, especially when they need help. The people telling you that isn't 100% correct, you must find a balance of what to listen to and what not to. The whole suck it up and be a man to hide your emotions is wrong; you need to vent. Think about a pressure cooker (for those old enough to remember them.) If you are cooking something and the pressure steam is building up, if the lid of the pot isn't removed, then the pot would shake or make a noise. Some people are just like that. If they can't vent to someone and release some steam or tension, then at some point in their lives, they will have a nervous breakdown, go crazy or do something that jeopardizes their freedom. We all need a support system, a therapist, a close circle, and a higher power to vent to. We need these outlets in life to process certain things. They can help you understand how you tick or how to help you make a better decision and help you avoid a seriously bad decision. You cannot do it alone; I have learned that myself. I just thank God I didn't end my life or risk my freedom to learn that. Seek help if you feel like you are running out of options; some bad decisions happen when you feel like there is no other way.

I love my wife, children, and my family and never want to disrespect their lives or their feelings. This is how I felt during the storms I was going through as well as the process to get through the storms and excel. I share my story because I know that someone needs to read it, hear about it, and help others by sharing it. The reasons for the delay in me writing this book now must become the reasons why I finish this book. I need to stop being selfish and share my journey, so others may believe they can move forward in their own journey. Understand that there is a way out of the storm, and it will require positive movement, tremendous help, and faith like no other. Everyone can survive the storms they face. This book can help with that. Every day that this book isn't out, someone could be losing and turning to a straitjacket instead of a Savior.

Chapter 1

The Need of a Savior

L et me start from the beginning. Back in the day, I went to a house party, but this wasn't just any old house party in DC. The vibes at this party seemed to be different, like this might be a really great night. The party was in a four-unit building; each unit played a part in the party. One unit was the coat check, the second unit was where drinks and wings were served, the third unit was the dance floor, and the fourth unit was where people were playing board games and watching TV. It was a dope party set up; I went with one of my boys and someone he knew. The funny thing about it was I only went because I didn't have to drive. While at this dope party, an attractive woman passed by my eyes, and I noticed that she was with her girlfriends but not really in their conversations. She just so happened to give me this look of please save me. At least in my mind, that's what I took it as. So, me being me, I had to introduce myself. I knew that once we started the conversation, along with the atmosphere being so positive that night, she would be hooked. Over some great and challenging years later, I was right; she is still with me. We have experienced a unique collection of challenges and championships in our dating relationship and marriage. I have done a ton of knucklehead things in our time together. But I have done more great things in times where my strength was needed for us both to continue breathing. My vision of marriage was totally different from my actual marriage. I have gone through some things in this marriage that would make anyone glad that I found a Savior over a straitjacket.

Challenges in life come in various forms. Some challenges will also be easy to spot, while others will operate in some form of stealth mode. This means you must do some serious searching to find the root of your challenge. The reason why I say these things is in today's time, I haven't always practiced what I posted. Valid reasons or not, there have been times where I lied to myself and tried to mask the challenge because of the work it would take to get past.

People try to oversell themselves because they think people need to hear that. Some portray fakeness as realness, and others follow and believe that. Both are mistaken and need to relax and be themselves, but in today's world, no one wants you to see their struggle. Being honest and self-aware is my way of injecting life and value into others. Talk to the world about your process when you are going through it more than the advice you think people want to hear. Speak to people, be human, don't allow outside factors to draw you away from helping. In my opinion, everyone has their own reasons for needing a Savior; some will even try to convince themselves that one doesn't exist. Some people will be so much in the midst of their own storms that they won't even know where to look.

I needed a Savior more than I ever thought I would. I was kind of cocky with myself, thinking I could do everything by myself. I was completely WRONG. Sometimes the reason I was in a mess mentality, physically or financially, was because I wasn't leaning on my Savior for guidance. That's the tricky part about needing a savior. You don't realize you need one until you have exhausted all the other options instead of looking to your Savior as the first option. God's plan might be to come to God first; then God will put the right people in place to assist you. I didn't start out that way, but after bumping my head a decent amount of times, I realized I needed my Savior. I think that was a difficult thing for me to realize that I needed help, and there wasn't anything wrong with needing or figuring out where to seek help. Help is not a disrespectful thing or word. Once you get through some life lessons alone, if you are blessed enough, you'll realize you need all the help you can get. Life isn't easy; if it's worth it, then you have to work for it.

How many times has an event or someone in your life disappointed you? That might be a difficult question to ask yourself, but the answers have to be found, causing you to have to show your work. It will require a ton of work, but the work will reward you. I say that because, at times, I have looked for the easy way to do something or wanted the reward without the work. Life doesn't work for everyone like that. If you want to win consistently, then you have to work your hardest consistently.

Always focus on improving; too many times, people quit right before the blessing. Then complain about things never working in their favor. Stop it; being alive is the ultimate blessing and what you do with that blessing is up to you. It's always easier said than done. Words always are easier than the execution of those words.

We all need a Savior or a higher power to look to for guidance, don't we? I say that because I don't know if everyone believes that. This world we live in has too many issues and sometimes not enough solutions.

Pain is something we all experience, but there are certain experiences that cause a different type of pain. Have you ever cried so much you get exhausted? The type of crying that keeps you from focusing on positive things. Have you ever cried like a baby as an adult to the point you get sleepy, but you feel so much pain and sadness that you can't fall asleep? I'm sure you might have, or at some point, if you live long enough, you might. Have you ever felt your heart drop or skip a beat but not from fear? We all have been in some dark places before, the kind that you'd never wish on your worst enemy.

Replaying the events back in my mind becomes stressful at times, but it also makes me focus on what my purpose in life should be. Why continue to wake up, and why go to work? Why, why, why? The reason why I continue is that I didn't want to end my life prematurely because people and myself would know that I ended my life because of something bad. I didn't want my end to come from these situations because it could have caused bigger ripple effects within my family or my wife's family. I knew that if God's plan for me was going to work, then I had to be around for it.

Chapter 2

Savior, Please Step In

I got married to my wife, and I couldn't believe I was going through with it. Before this point, I really thought I would be a bachelor for at least many more years, but life doesn't always work out like that. My parents and friends were happy with me getting married. I was one of the few of my friends that were married and the only child my parents had that was married. I can remember my parents just smiling from ear to ear, just so overwhelmed with joy and happiness. I have made my parents proud on many occasions in my life, but on my wedding day, they seemed the happiest. Seeing my parents, this happy made me want to keep them this way forever.

Not even married for a year, my son Jamison was born. He was a healthy and strong baby boy. My parents were even happier that they now have a grandchild than they were at my wedding. I didn't even think that was possible. Finally, seeing my son was surreal because I still had a baby face, let alone having a baby. The Lord works in mysterious ways. I didn't know having my son would be a peak at that time in my family's life. Once my son, Jamison, was born, my parents wanted me to come to visit even more, and they started visiting even more just to see my wife and

Jamison. I asked them, "What about me?" My mom said, "Boy, we raised you; we know you well." My mom and Jamison would always smile at one another all the time. It seemed like they were connected by a kindred spirit. The conversations that I was having with my parents had a different sound to them. We talked about the role of being a parent how a baby can affect a marriage, good or bad, among other things that wouldn't have happened had I not been a parent. The level of appreciation for my parents has grown a great deal since now I can share stories with them about being a parent. Some of the advice they had given me as a child was making a ton of sense now that I had a child. Everything was going amazing, I got used to being a parent, and with all the sleepless nights and crying, there are way more amazing things about being a dad. Thanksgiving rolled around, and Jamison, Tiffany, and I visited my parents and extended family. We drove to Brooklyn, NY, to a traditional family dinner. Aunts, cousins, uncles, friends all wanted to see Jamison. He was very young at that time, one month old or so. Everyone wanted to hold him or just watch me hold him and give me advice on how to love and protect him. It was an amazing holiday, one that I will never forget. Now for that Christmas, we flew to Houston, TX, to visit my wife's family since it was our first Christmas as a new family. We had a blast out there in H-town; I remember the weather being very warm on Christmas Day, 75 degrees. The warmest Christmas I ever witnessed, since I was born and raised in NYC, the warmest Christmas might have been 40 something degrees. Talk about a total shock; I didn't even know that was possible. I wasn't mad at the warmer weather at all, but just surprised Christmas could be that warm. We had a great time, Tiffany's family was super cool to be around, and they know how to really cook. A couple of times, I asked if Mrs. Granville (my mom) was in the kitchen helping them cook. My mom and Tiffany's aunts must have been sisters in another life because they cooked in extremely similar styles. I just kept thinking of how one day I'm going to plan something, so my side of the family and Tiffany's side of the family could get together and just have fun. This was a Christmas for the ages, the first one in the South, the first time around most of my wife's family, and the first one as a parent with my wife. The list goes on.

We visit my parents more often, and they visit us as well, just giving us the game on how to parent and tips and love. A few months later, though, unexpectedly, my mom was in the hospital. I would visit her every weekend. I would bring smiles and pictures of her grandson, Jamison, every weekend with this digital photo frame that one of my friends gave me as a wedding gift. Seeing how my mom's face would light up when she saw pictures of Jamison smiling but getting older and bigger, I knew she was fighting cancer as best as she could. She would always tell me to keep bringing pictures cause it helps. Also, she never wanted Jamison to come to visit because hospitals have too many germs, and she didn't want him getting any. Look at mom always being a mom; she was always very protective and loving of her family. She told me not to come to visit her on Father's Day weekend because she said this is your first one and you don't need to be in any hospital. She told me to come the following weekend but make sure I take a ton of pictures. Who knew that would be my first Father's Day weekend with Mom and Jamison not being together? That weekend I was able to spend with Jamison and my wife. It was my first Father's Day ever; I was super excited but tried to play it cool. I remember that day as if it was yesterday, it was the clearest sky possible with few clouds, but they were whiter than chalk. Even though we went to a BBQ spot, and I wore a white polo shirt and tan shorts, not an ounce of BBQ sauce got on my outfit. I think I should get extra points for that; how often does that happen? We took tons of pictures inside the BBQ spot, in an elevator, but especially by a huge water fountain. The water fountain would allow Jamison to really show his personality. He was making similar faces as me and smiling so much; I knew mom would love these photos. I was praying that by seeing how much life, Jamison was showing, she would beat cancer. We took so many pictures, and Jamison smiled so much; he was so happy. He didn't cry at all that day. Normally, babies cry a little bit, but not that day; it's almost like he knew if he smiled for Grandma, then it would help her get better.

On the weekend of July 4th, my dad called me and said, "Christopher, how soon can you get to New York?" Normally, my dad doesn't call me by my full name unless I'm in trouble. I said, "What's up, dad? Is everything okay?" "Get here as fast and as safe as possible," he said and hung up right after. I knew something was wrong but didn't know for sure. My wife had family in town that weekend and my dad knew, but if he called me and said that, then I have to excuse myself and get to New York ASAP. I drove to New York as swift and safe as possible. I drove straight to the hospital, not knowing for sure that's where my dad wanted me to go. But the more I thought about how my dad's tone sounded; I knew something was wrong. I got to the hospital, and I saw other family members there, as well as a pastor. I saw everyone sitting by my mom's bedside, just with a cloud of sadness over them like I had never seen before. My mom was just lying in her bed, but this time, she was connected to a machine. I looked at everyone, then at this machine mom was connected to, and realized it's a life support machine. I just started to cry, but at first, no tears came down, then as I continued to step closer to my mom, the tears came down my face like a waterfall. I just thought to myself, how come I didn't even get a chance to say goodbye to her? The life support machine was only there because mom had transitioned to Heaven, and physically her body was there, but her soul had moved on.

July 4th, my mom died. She was called home to be with the Lord. I was sad, upset but happy she wasn't suffering from cancer anymore. At my mom's funeral, there were so many people there who she had made an impact on; there were about a thousand people there. I saw people I knew and people I had never met, but they all had similar stories about how positive and funny my mom was to be around. The things I already knew but was blessed to know that God allowed her to have an impact on so many lives besides my own. Even though it was such a sad time, Jamison was there, and everyone marveled at his smile and how much he looked like mom. People were saying, oh, now I see why she was so happy; look at her handsome grandchild; he looks just like her. Jamison just looked at everyone and smiled as if he knew who they were and what they were talking about. Even though times were difficult and painful, God has a way of using people to show that happier times do exist. Losing a parent is **hard** especially being so unexpected. I wanted my mom to be alive forever. She just became a grandparent; she had so much more life to live and so much love she could teach and show Jamison. My father was really affected by my mom's death as well; he is one of the strongest men I've ever met and lost his wife; my mom was the type of blow that hit him like a ton of bricks. Losing mom took a visible and invisible toll on all of us.

Later that summer, while I was almost off from work, I noticed that I had a voicemail on my work phone. I didn't think anything of it because only a few people have my work number, so no big deal. But little did I know that it would be a life-changing voicemail. It was a voicemail from a detective saying to call him as soon as possible. I thought, what in the world, but I called back, and I could tell from the detective's voice that whatever I was doing prior or planning to do wasn't nearly as important as getting to the hospital he was at. The detective told me to leave work and get to the hospital as fast and as safe as possible. My mind was racing a hundred miles an hour, but I had to remain focused on the road. Why did the detective need me to get to the hospital? What happened? I tried calling Tiffany several times but no answer. But in the back of my mind, the tone in the detective's voice sounded just like the tone in my dad's voice when he wanted me to get to New York when my mom passed away. But I'm like, nah, nothing that serious could have happened again in two months. I activated prayer mode while driving, hopeful that it was nothing too serious. The hospital was about twenty-five minutes from my job, but I got there in about ten minutes. I wasn't running any red lights, but I wasn't stopping at yellow lights either. I got to the hospital, looking for information, and I was told where to go. Little did I know that behind those hospital doors was going to be my biggest test. Tiffany was sitting in the ER room, crying uncontrollably, holding Jamison. At first, in my mind, I wondered what was going on? As I got closer to them, I noticed Jamison wasn't moving, almost like he was sleeping. Tiffany was crying more and more and told me Jamison was dead. My heart just dropped; I cried like never before. I just cried the most in my life when my mom died two months prior. By this point, now I'm crying way more than that, to the point it affected my breathing. I sat down and asked my wife and the doctors what had happened. He was a healthy baby boy and was about to turn eleven months in a week. There weren't any issues at his last routine doctor visit. They told me Jamison died at daycare in his sleep and that he didn't suffer. I felt at this moment that my Savior was pulling on me while the straitjacket was pulling just as strong. Why? Who did I anger? Why did this have to be the punishment? I said to God, why break me down even further? You made your point when you called my mom home. What did I do to disrespect the kingdom that this was payback? I just remember my mom saying when I was younger that you shouldn't question God, but now I think I do need to question. My mom was the strongest believer I knew, and she was gone, and now my only child was gone. How do I make sane decisions? Why shouldn't I just check out now, mentally check out? Physically checking out was on the table for sure. This could be my straitjacket moment that would change my life for the worst. I just also thought that maybe just maybe, Jamison couldn't pass before my mom because his passing might have been the thing that would have killed her. So, my mind was just spinning a million miles an hour. I must stay strong for my wife now because we created Jamison together, but she carried him inside of her, so I know she is most likely more mentally messed up than myself. If I turn to a straitjacket and check out mentally or physically, she might do the same. I can't let that happen right now. As much as I'm hurting, I can't be selfish. How do I make sense of all of this sadness and pain? How do I continue to carry on?

Losing mom and especially now Jamison, I was at my lowest moment. I knew I was in such a dark space, but I didn't realize how dark of a space I was in. Have you ever cried so much you get exhausted? This is the type of crying that keeps you from focusing on positive things. Have you ever cried like a baby as an adult, cried to the point you get sleepy? But you feel so much pain and sadness that you can't fall asleep?

I cried like that in the shower every night for almost a year straight; I didn't want anyone to know that I was breaking down mentally and emotionally. When I was around people, I tried to speak as strongly as possible cause I knew I was going to cry once I got into the shower. That also was my time to be alone and try to figure things out. I didn't think my Savior wanted anything to do with me and that checking out mentally or physically would be the best option. I was getting closer to finding out how to get put into a mental home. I felt like I needed a straitjacket just to feel better. I felt like I was going to check out from reality.

But I remember my mom always saying to me whenever times got difficult when I was younger that God would never leave you nor forsake you. Meaning God is always going to look out for you, but God works on God's time and not mine. I felt like if God really cared, then this would have never happened, but the more I said that, the more I realized that's not how my mom would want me to think. Also, how do I honor mom and Jamison by staying in this dark place that doesn't help anyone? Me thinking about how to honor my lost loved ones was a real help for me in moving toward my Savior over a straitjacket. Prayer, more prayer, therapy, and being around positive people also helped me get out and stay out of the darkest moment in my life. If you are or anyone you know is feeling like there is no way out, please seek help.

Jamison at 10 months old.

Chapter 3

You Never Know

I say all of that to say this; I lost two extremely important people in my life within two months of one another. How do you get knocked down twice before you realize what's going on? How do you get knocked down a second time before you can get up from the first knock-down? That's not fair, that's illegal in sports, but life isn't a sport- it's a journey. There are no timeouts or days off, you can go on vacation, but life continues. No matter the pain, no matter the situation, you have to stay strong but pray stronger. Finding the strength to continue on is sometimes the biggest challenge of all. It's too easy to quit, get lazy, being an inactive participant in your own life because you got hit with some adversity without warning. The sad part is, for a while, I felt like this; I just was in a dark place. Parts of me wanted to stay there forever, but I knew that wouldn't be best for myself or my remaining family.

Mark 9:23 NLT

"What do you mean, 'If I can?'" Jesus asked. "Anything is possible if a person believes."

That verse is difficult to live with when you are going through a storm, but much needed reinforcement in order to get through the storm.

I understand God has a plan for everyone, but I wish I could go over the plan and tweak some parts of the plan with God. I know for sure that my mother and son dying soon would have been tweaked for sure without question. How come we couldn't discuss those two events first or have debated or had at least heard my reasons why I wouldn't have gone with those things. I would have tried my best to talk God out of letting those things happen. Like take my life but spare their lives or how about you let us all live together so we can be happy. Or hear out my family's reasons for those events not occurring at those times. Faith gets tested, but only with faith can you pass the test. Not even sure if passing the test is what is needed, maybe more like understanding why you have to be tested in the first place.

Why did I want to breathe and continue with my life after being hit with two tragic losses in a two-month span? How do I look people in the eyes? Why would I want to? How do I look at myself in the mirror? What can anyone tell me to make me feel better? I heard from people that I never knew as well as people who I thought I knew not wanting to speak to me using the excuse (might have been valid in their minds) *'I didn't know what to say. I'm so sorry for your loss; be strong.'* I'm sure people meant, well, but I didn't want to hear them. All these statements and more were said to me, and so many not-so-favorable responses were going through my head. Some of them still go through my head when speaking to people about the subject. I understand that in order to get through things, you have to go through some things. I now gauge my conversations with people differently, before I would share my positive experiences or moments all the time; now, I don't as much. I try not to ask people about their kids, or if they have any, I use statements like how's the fam? Or is everything good? Instead of asking for details, I tend to generalize my conversations. Unless they share first, I tend not to press them about certain things. You just don't know who is going through something that they might not be prepared to talk about or know how to take your responses.

The crazy part about it is my son, Jamison, was born on 10/23, and he died ten months and twenty-three days later. That's some BS, God. I was disappointed in God's decision, but I know there have been way more times I let God down, so I knew my day was coming but not like this. Why did this have to happen? I still wonder why to this day. The timing of things happens regardless of if you have planned for them or not. I can't wait to ask, though, if I'm able to. I wasn't the best dad ever, but I was a great, amazing, awesome dad that was present every day and tried not to make any excuses. But God felt it was best for everyone that Jamison passing away was necessary at that time. My mind bounced around from time to time; thinking about those days before these events, I was more engaged in my thoughts. What if these events didn't happen? Where would my life be? Would blessings still happen? How come my mom and son couldn't co-exist with my other children and family? Why couldn't I have learned the important lessons with them still being here? I know this may sound selfish but, in this situation, I want to be selfish cause I could still use their positive energy from both of them. I know if I ever get to meet my Savior and be able to have a conversation with him, I can envision our conversation going a little something like, I appreciate you letting me through the pearly gates, but why did you take my mom and Jamison when you did? God, couldn't you have pushed their deaths back a few decades? What path was I going down that you didn't warrant them being there? Not just my path but everyone that was affected by their passing. Did they do something wrong to you that no one knew about? Not sure when or if I will get to have those questions answered at all.

During those times, I tried to focus but didn't care as much because I kept going back to how different things could have been.

People experience various amounts of stress and frustrations at all levels in their normal day-to-day lives. I don't know the 'textbook' way to deal with grief; not sure there is one. Everyone deals with loss in their own way; I was dealing with two losses while trying to keep my marriage together. You hear stories about people losing their close family members unexpectedly or some other tragedies, but I never thought I would be that person. Losing my mom and son within two months felt like the ultimate tragedy.

Who could relate? Who would want to relate to this even? No one walks around with a sign on their forehead. Even when I write this stuff down, my mind races around all over the place. I had to find hope and help.

I will use the positive characteristics from my mom and son and instill that into my life from here on out. Both were always cheerful and light in any dark space. Maybe God's plan is for me to do those things. Hopefully, I can use this tragedy to inspire others. Hopefully, by finding my Savior, I can keep others from turning to a straitjacket.

Jamison at 7 months old

Chapter 4

Mindset Shifting

My wife and I have always had the ambition to help others, but we didn't know exactly how we would. Even though I grew up as the youngest of three children, I always felt I could relate and help others regardless of my age. Be a servant to people and assist in making their dreams come true. So many times, in my youth and adult life, I have helped people who, for whatever reasons, weren't in a position to help themselves, and I say that not looking for a pat on the back but just to let people know that I'm a helper. If I can help, I will, even if sometimes it really doesn't make sense to help the person. You never know the path God has for you. Who knew that I would have to face two extreme tragedies in order to start helping people differently from the past? Especially kids that experience loss as well. (Some actually physically and some just because of irresponsibility and neglect.)

This is where my mindset started to shift; I knew if I appreciated what my mom and Jamison did for me, then I needed to help more people .than I could imagine. We were a newly married couple that had already faced much sadness that could derail any marriage no matter the time together. We had talked about how to help people, marriage, life, and other serious topics that we needed to discuss in order to make it out of this dark place.

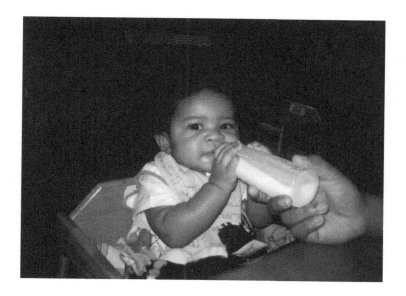

Jamison is eating on Father's Day

Chapter 5
Change Happens Through Actions

B elow is taken from//www.umfs.org/virginia-foster-care-statistics /Current Foster Care Statistics

Many children come into foster care each year. Consider these foster care statistics as you learn more about the foster care system in Virginia and across the United States. National Numbers

- There are approximately **440,000 children** in foster care across the United States. (Adoption and Foster Care Analysis Report, August 2018 AFCARS)

- The average age of a foster child in the U.S. is **8 years old**. (ACF)The average length of time a child resides in foster care in the U.S in **12 months**. (ACF)

- **50% percent** of U.S. children in foster care will be reunited with their parents or primary caregiver. (ACF)

- There are approximately **125,000 children** in foster care in the U.S. who are waiting for adoption. (ACF)

- Nearly **60,000 children** in foster care in the U.S. get adopted each year. (ACF)

- **25% percent** of children in foster care are adopted, often by their foster parents. (ACF)**20,000 children** in foster care age out of the system at age 18 or 21. (ACF)

- **20%** of teens who age out of foster care will **become instantly homeless.** (National Foster Youth Institute)

- **70%** of the young women who age out of foster care **become pregnant before 21.** (National Foster Youth Institute)

Being a foster/ resource parent at a young age is not a common thing at all. You get the people asking the following questions or similar statements:

"OH, what, you can't have kids? "

"Well, it's not the same as having your own kids."

"You are too young to do that."

"Why wouldn't you have your own kids first before doing that? "

"Are you going to have more kids? "

"Aren't you afraid you will get too attached to those kids? "

"What made you want to become a foster parent? "

Little do people realize I already had a child and that doing this doesn't stop that. We even went to foster care seminars even while Jamison was alive, so it was on our hearts for some time. You can multitask, in this case, foster and still try to have biological kids. I totally understand what people were saying. I refuse to be defined by *failure* and loss; I'm a winner, a success story. Why do this? How are you so sure you like kids that much? Especially kids that know you are not their father or the fact that you are the only man they that has shown support for them. They will disappoint you, and you will disappoint them. When dealing with younger and older kids, you have to find a way to be a positive part of their life in such a short time frame. Too many kids, especially foster kids, go through their life without having a positive male in their life. That is a shame, men, we need to step up, and I need to step up. I won't allow myself to watch kids fall by the wayside just because they are not my kids. Those kids might become my enemy later in life if they turn to a life of crime all possible because I didn't spend some positive time with them when they needed it most. Not on my watch, I will do my best to try to help all kids I encounter. People helped me become a better person, so I will work on doing the same. The process isn't easy, but we all know the saying 'anything worth doing won't always be easy to do. 'When Tiffany and I really became serious about becoming foster parents, we went to various agencies. One we went to was for people wanting only infants whether they were from this country or not. We thought that was honorable, but not for us at the time. The next agency we went to told us that we should just deal with our loss and wait longer to apply even though the process of becoming a resource/ foster parent takes months, sometimes years. When we asked them the time frame of how long we should wait, they told us there was no exact time frame, but a year would be good. So, I'm like, why and who are you to tell me that I need to wait to help? It's not like people are storming the gates to line up and help, not to sound bad. But there are too many kids in need of help, and you are telling us to wait, but you don't have an exact time frame. They told us to get through all the holidays and birthdays first then come back. We said to the agency how they would know that we are the best people after one year, and is it one year from our loss or one year from speaking to them? Again, they didn't have a concrete response. So even when trying to do better, you will face challenges, but God rewards those who work in faith and prayer inside their hearts. Well, I always remember hearing a saying that NO just means next opportunity. If Tiffany and I can't become foster parents now, then maybe later in life. One day at church, we heard during the announcements that they were going to have a speaker from a faith-based foster agency. So, Tiffany and I decided to go; maybe it would be different, maybe not.

But if we don't go, we will never know. So, we spoke to this new agency, and they said similar things that could have been roadblocks, but we were focused and knowledgeable, so we asked better questions. We asked about the possibility of being checked out by a therapist. Foster kids have to see therapists because of the trauma and loss they experience, so why can't a prospective foster parent do the same? This agency was fine with that because the process of becoming a foster parent takes time. Just because we suffered extreme losses doesn't mean we can't help people. We might relate to these kids more than other people because of our loss. Kids don't like being alone or feeling like no one understands them, which is the feeling we feel at times. Every new opportunity will present us with different challenges, but we were built to do better; the losses of mom and Jamison are a motivation for us to help others. I try to find my inner strength from how I handled my past failures or bumps in life.

Mentally, trying to revisit the moment I realized the failure and got through it. You always have to update or upgrade your technology; why not upgrade yourself? While we were going to go through this process with the faith-based agency, we decided to become mentors for older foster kids aged ten and up. We found out about this big brother/sister program through the internet, or someone told us about it. This program was just a mentor program; you would spend time with the kids for a few hours one Saturday a month. This program gave the kids a break from their foster parents and also allowed us to figure out if we really wanted to become foster parents or just do this monthly mentorship. This monthly mentorship was totally different and had nothing to do with actually becoming a foster parent.

Jamison smiling at my parent's house

Chapter 6
Challenges of Change

The process of change is an upgrade from chatter. Everyone can chatter, but not everyone can change. Too many people chatter about change, but the people that change don't chatter too much. There is no testimony without a test; you can't be for the better if you don't work toward that change. Failure shouldn't be enough for you to quit if you believe God is working with you. Prayer and faith are going to help us as we embark on this journey called life. The energy it takes to change is far greater than the energy it takes to chatter about change. Life would be so much easier if we could just chatter about the change, but would life still be so precious if things worked without work? Techniques and brainstorming about change sound great, but the execution is respected change. Failure is a part of the change; going down the road less traveled is a part of changing for the better. The process of changing will make you feel like quitting or just becoming an inactive participant in your own life. I talk about change because that's what I had to do in order to stay out of a straitjacket. I was in a dark place that I wouldn't want to wish on my worst enemy. I had to rebuild my mental state what seemed like from scratch once Jamison and mom passed away. The things I thought I learned in my life up until that point I felt like it didn't apply to me. My mental state was the biggest transformation even when I physically didn't feel like moving.

I can never be your "birth father," but I may be the only father-like person you may have met or even dealt with. If I can save one or help one child become a better person, then the time and energy used to help are never wasted. Some of these kids, in my experience, test you because you are the 'new guy,' or why do you care? No other person wanted to see them become successful. I want all kids to be the best they can be, but in order to be better, you're going to have to work *extremely* hard because your previous life experiences might've not helped much. Everyone wants to be great, but not everyone wants to work like the greats. The process of becoming better is just that a process. I can never relate to being in a foster home or broken home, but I understand that in order to be great, you have to outwork whatever your negative situation is/was. Sometimes luck happens, but prayer and practice can become permanent tools to succeed; learning and following directions help as well. Challenge people respectfully, meaning provide people with the facts and build off of that. Every person deals with loss and hurt in their own way, but don't dwell on those issues, use them as fuel and motivation to do better. I say these things almost every day to remind myself that this path isn't for everyone. The qualities that my mom and Jamison shared with me I will share with people. Hopefully, they will see that I just want to help others win. Don't be defined by pain or suffering. Instead, be defined by the triumph and the successful feeling once you look back at where you were before the win.

Our past experiences sometimes assist in defining our future. But I always remember my dad telling me, 'What good is knowledge if you don't share it?' So, I use my past and want more knowledge to help strengthen my future. So, I cannot be defined by my loss because I look for inspiration, knowing my rock bottom. These were hopefully my lowest points in life, and I never want to experience that again. So, I feel prepared to help kids who, at the time of meeting me, might only see themselves as defined by their losses. Don't look at the glass as half-empty; look at it as half full. I tell kids to look at how strong they are and how much stronger they can become. The future is brighter now that they can dream and experience better days; once a kid is exposed to better things, they have a greater chance of accomplishing better things. Changing the mindset is the challenge; they have been losing for so long that they don't believe they can start winning.

In my experiences with mentoring and spending time with kids, whether foster or non-foster kids, I started to realize everyone is nervous when they first meet someone. For example, on the first day at school, the mind starts to wonder if you can make friends, are kids going to laugh at me, or will people like me? Some kids in foster care experience nervousness or fear all the time. New family, old family future is uncertain, having to go to new schools, new social workers, new therapists, the list goes on and on. Nowhere mentioned is a stable environment because if a place becomes stable, then a child might be moved for various reasons. Life is challenging, but life doesn't care if a child is in foster care or a picture-perfect home; time keeps moving forward regardless.

I have talked to some older foster children and tried my best to give them information, resume help, sneakers, talked to them about spirituality, a testimony, an ear so they can vent. So, they will understand that life doesn't care about your past, but life also will give you help even if it doesn't come with a visible sign. Also, people will cross your path in life, sometimes to help and sometimes to hate. I tell them to pay attention to people and their behavior when they are around various people and to watch their hand movements. Hand movement is extremely important. It is a non-verbal communicator and a form of body language. I remember my dad telling me as a kid to watch how people use their hands because looks can't kill; hands can. Also, depending on hand movement, you can get a better gauge on if someone likes you.

I didn't know what strength was until I was going through my storm and still was pushing to help others out of their own. I just was doing what I felt was right or what I thought someone would do for me. Growing up, people helped me out so, and I didn't succeed alone. No one wins alone, and no one loses alone. A team can help or hurt your progress in life no matter what. Some teams are not a good fit for you, some last only a season, some last forever. Keep reminding yourself that the comeback is better than the setback. I know I can never get my mom and Jamison back in the physical form, but I have faith that I will see and hug them in the spiritual form as long as I continue to follow God's plan.

Every gift from God takes work, even in simple terms, a child is born, and in order to develop to become an adult, they have to work to become the best they can be. Every day is a process, and you have to grind to become great each day. So, there will be challenges and issues that will appear, but you have to be strong enough to continue to grind. Don't accept the life you have been given; grind until you create the life you've been dreaming about. But also grind with a vision, or in other words, you need to have the vision to reinforce the intensity of your grind. I say this because I see so many kids in the foster care system that had dreams but going from home to home has forced their dreams to vanish or be forgotten about. They are just grinding to survive, using the energy that a stable home environment would normally provide so they can focus on other things; they don't have a stable environment. So, they can't chill and relax; they have to move from home to home whether they behave badly or not. Not every child moves to various homes, but I can only imagine how I would have felt if I had to move from my home and family as a kid. Not every kid endures years of neglect, but the kids that do, I pray for them sometimes more than anyone else. No matter the kid, whether foster child or not, it takes time to develop into a successful and responsible person. Stability plays a huge role in a child's success. Imagine what your life would look like if your childhood were unstable. Without a stable home or positive environment, success appears even more unlikely. What kid doesn't want friends, what adult doesn't want stable friends, or someone to talk to? Unfortunately, some kids in foster care don't have that stability, moving from home to home having to reinvent themselves. Not knowing who you really are because a stable environment would help build that knowledge of yourself. Survival mode kicks in so much that once they find that stable place, they don't even realize it. In my experience with having foster kids, having them realize that my home is safe and they are now in a stable environment is a day-to-day challenge. Foster kids have come to my home with trash bags as suitcases and tell me that they didn't even say goodbye to the people at the last home they came from. In some cases, they woke up in the morning thinking everything was sweet, and while at school, the previous foster parent and social worker were trying to find a new foster home for the kid. Crazy, crazy situation, isn't it? They envision going home to their home then being told that's not their home anymore. Then they're taken to another home for the unforeseeable future.

Mindset is the key; with the wrong mindset, some would have been in a straitjacket, jailed or dead a long time ago. But God isn't finished with you, so you must strengthen your mindset. Improving my mindset allowed me to accept the challenges with an open mind and hunger to tackle anything. Continue to pray to think about your actions before doing them. Reading books more about self-help or empowerment has been an asset to my mental state and can be for you as well. Helping people is all we want to do, the same thing my mom and Jamison were known to do.

I've heard some very unfortunate stories from social workers and kids as foster parents. I always tried to be compassionate because of this. How can life be considered easier to some and not others? When you are faced with adverse events, I believe the inner champion has to show up, or you will fold.

God placed me in challenging times before; dealing with loss is just a newer unwanted challenge. Growing up in a household where both parents played an active role in my life helped me deal with the trauma. I think my mother having such a great belief in God and always praying over her children has helped me continue to live. I had to take a special part of her life and experiences and add them to my life to honor her. I believe in order to pay tribute to our loved ones who are no longer in the physical form; we have to incorporate special things about them into our lives. So, when new people meet you, they'll know there's something special about you. No matter how difficult any situation is, you have to have faith and work to get help in gaining some sanity in your life. I cannot stress enough the importance of prayer and memories as well as therapy. Too many lives can be saved; continue to push on and honor their lives by adding happy things into yours.

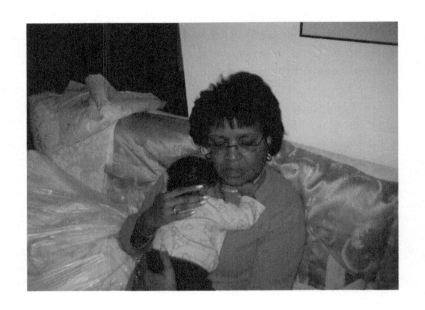

Jamison and my mom

Chapter 7

Old Life vs. New Life

I have a tremendous number of things on my plate; some things don't pay, but they weigh heavily on my mental health. Some things on my plate are there just to keep me productive, while others might be just taking up space. How can I add value to someone else's life if I am battling my own struggles? My dad used to always tell me, "What good is information if you don't share it?" I said, "Isn't applied information what you mean?" He replied, "How can you apply information if you don't know the information exists?" Parents always have an answer for everything. So, as I've gotten older, I have shared my knowledge with people, and they can apply it if they choose. This thinking applies to me while I am telling my complex life to whoever reads this book. My old, carefree life only lasted for some time, I grew up in an amazing two-parent home which wasn't perfect, but my parents didn't believe in a plan B. They made sacrifices, had arguments, had their differences with one another, but they didn't divorce one another. They were still married when my mom passed away on July 4th. I say that to say this, not everyone is going to be married for a long time or even get married, but if you have a child or children, you have to make sure both parents are respected. Even if they get on your last nerve, just out of respect for the lens, the child will view their parents. Respect is key. So, I grew up with respect for marriage but also respect for people in a relationship or former relationship. I haven't always done the best in my relationships at all, but because of my parents' verbal and non-verbal treatment of one another, I didn't sway away too much. They had a unified front when it came to their children; not one of us kids would break my parents' bond. Even if we thought we could convince one parent to believe in the kids' side of the story, they didn't fall for it. They stayed united in the treatment of the kids; whether it was punishments or praises, they were together. As a child, I paid attention and noticed that in my adulthood. My old life had a foundation of that through thick and thin; marriage should work; if you have doubts, then stay single. No plan B, but losing my mom and Jamison in a two-month span for sure put that to the ultimate test. This is where having a Savior, prayer, and patience play a unique factor in staying married. I didn't want to feel like I was going to be broken and let my parents down if I decided to divorce because this pain I was feeling was my rock bottom. This rock bottom didn't feel right at all; days seemed like the blink of an eye. Tears that could fill up water coolers, the rejection that felt like too much to bear. Prayer and patience had helped me to just breathe and cry my way through if need be. *He will never leave you nor forsake you.* I needed to read that verse Hebrews 13:5 to keep from going and staying in dark spaces. It was and still is a challenge that has only moved me from an old life to a new life.

New life had begun - it got off to a slow and rocky start, but just like an infant, you will have trouble in the beginning but have to stay the course in order to figure things out. As you mature, things will become less painful to handle, I kept asking God if this were the way my life would end, and I believe God kept telling me he would never leave me and be patient. His plan wasn't for me to stop living but to start living. There will be more challenges, none this painful, but they will involve pain rest assured. In my mind, through conversations with God, I believed in this. Patience and prayer will allow you to deal with pain as well as troubling times. The grind doesn't stop unless you quit, and I wasn't going to quit on my marriage, family, God, or my life.

This chapter is called old life vs. new life because of the changes I had to go through. But anyone reading this can or should go through it if they are looking for significant change in their life. Caterpillars don't become butterflies without changing the old life into the new life. A **Muhammad Ali quote that I remember growing up said: "A man** who views the world the **same** at fifty as he did at twenty has wasted thirty years of his life." I interpreted it as meaning if you don't transition from an old way of thinking/living to a new way once you get older, then you are missing out on the importance of living. There was another quote I heard that made a ton of sense to me. Once I heard it, having already made my transition into a new life, it might not have made sense if I still was stuck in my old life. It was said: "I would have went insane had I remained the same me." (**Jay-Z quote**)

I know these quotes were for different circumstances, but I feel that they apply with the concept of growth, and growth will require changes. Whether it's spiritual, physical, mental, friendships, proximity, the list goes on. But we'll have to make changes if we want to grow.

Our First Father's Day

Chapter 8
Years Turn into Tears

It's been some time since Jamison died. Now even after all this time, I still think about how he would have looked, how he would have bonded with his other siblings. Man, I still wonder how come God didn't allow Jamison to still be around with everything we have going on. So many things go through my mind today, at times causing me to just sit back and be still. I am actually writing this chapter on the anniversary of his passing, just reflecting on his life the impact Jamison had on me. I was a young dad who was still wet behind the ears but loved just coming home from work and seeing his smile. Picking him up from daycare was always cool because when he saw me, he would smile so bright, and I did the same. No matter what type of day I had, Jamison always put a smile on my face. That's one thing I do now smile more because of him. These years seem like a blur at times; different moments throughout these last few years don't even seem real.

My life doesn't feel real sometimes because I can remember so many moments with Jamison as if they happened ten minutes ago. I try to take pictures with my other children, if not every day, then every week, just because if God calls them home earlier than me, then I want to have pictures that can assist with me remembering what we were doing in those pictures. The fun we were having or telling a story about the picture. They say a picture is worth a thousand words, and I truly believe that because every time I look at my youngest son Elijah, I see Jamison. They have so many similar features but are so different. Maybe God wanted Jamison and Elijah to look so much alike that every time I see Elijah, I would see Jamison. God does work in mysterious ways so, you never know. Prayer has been a reoccurring thing in my life since Jamison's passing because it is easier to be mad and mope around than it is to be appreciative and active. I am blessed to be able to have multiple children since Jamison's passing; not everyone that has experienced child loss can say the same thing. Count your blessings, people, not pain that might have happened before the blessings.

Chapter 9
The Honeymoon Period

Shortly before Jamison's passing, we started mentoring; then, after his passing, we started fostering. In total, we collectively worked with around fifty-plus kids. Many great moments, as well as some learning experiences, helped us deal with the next Savior instead of a straitjacket moment. After a few years, we must make a detour.

My life has changed drastically since mom and Jamison have passed. Tiffany and I have become foster parents as well as renewed parents. We have our three children, and we now have my mother-in-law, my dad, and my grandfather (mom's dad) living with us. Eight of us live in a single-family home where everyone has their own space. Never have we thought when we purchased another home that God was planning for us to have this crib filled with a new family as well as an old family. Multiple generations are now living with us; wow, that's something you hear about from other races or stories your parents or grandparents have shared. Thank God we have multiple bathrooms and multiple levels, or that would be trouble. Whether it's a non-biological or biological family, I believe Tiff and I are doing what God has planned for us. We are helpers, and we have troubles just like everyone else, but we have been dealt a hand that not everyone has to hold. So, helping families won't be anywhere near as challenging as dealing with extreme loss. A person can pretend to care, but you can't pretend to show up and help others in need. Our families and others appreciate our stepping up, but most don't want to do what we do. We want to change someone's life improve people's mindset; I want everyone to succeed because if you succeed, then I know my mother and Jamison are smiling. My wife and I don't feel right if we don't help people. If you are ever able to be in a position to help anyone, I recommend doing it, but it will require some level of maturity that you may or may not have at the time you commit to stepping up. Be prepared because you will get attacked by others/things who won't help. Be ready.

On this visit, my dad told me that he didn't want to go back home while he was visiting me. I asked him why not? He said because he didn't feel right and it would be just too much confusion for him. Not sure what that all meant, but none less dad needed help. The crazy part about it was my family and I had just come from Charlotte, NC, to visit my mom's father, who is my grandfather. My grandfather was planning to move to my home to be around family. Crazy how God works, my mom and him never really had a great relationship when she was alive, but she was happy that at least one of her children could have a different experience with him than she did. I know she must be smiling from heaven now. It was a decision that Tiff and I had to agree on. Granddad is cool, but how will he be in a house full of people. But the relationship he and I had, and the numerous visits I had with him, I knew our feelings were mutual that he needed to come live with us. Also, Tiffany has known and interacted with him for most of our marriage. In his elderly years, no one should be alone, plus my kids can bond with him for as long as God allows it. We are not perfect people, granddad is not a perfect person, but things don't have to be perfect in order to work. He is a quiet person that likes to stay to himself and walks to the beat of his own drum. Captain Cool Breeze is what we call him. He doesn't look his age and doesn't dress his age, so when people see him, they think he is my dad and not my grandfather, lol. He is cooler than an AC breeze, for sure.

To have so many people in this crib is a true adjustment. But I thank God every day that the house can fit everyone without people being on top of one another. The different personalities working together under one roof are pretty unique. Even though no one is in the house alone ever, it still takes some time to get used to having so many people around.

Proverbs 18:1 Whoever isolates himself seeks his own desire; he breaks out against all sound judgment.

Proverbs 20:11 Even small children are known by their actions, so is their conduct really pure and upright?

Psalm 41:9 Even my close friend, someone I trusted, one who shared my bread, has turned against me.

Proverbs 27:6 Do not take advantage of each other,

Luke 8:17 For all that is secret will eventually be brought into the open, and everything that is concealed will be brought to light and made known to all.

Galatians 6:2 "Bear one another burdens, and so fulfill the law of Christ.

Titus 2:2, NLT: "Teach the older men to exercise self-control, to be worthy of respect, and to live wisely. They must have sound faith and be filled with love and patience.

Galatians 6:7 Do not be deceived: God is not mocked, for whatever one sows, that will he also reap.

Proverbs 13:1A wise son hears his father's instruction, but a scoffer does not listen to rebuke.

Proverbs 11:2When pride comes, then comes shame; but with the humble is wisdom.

These verses are encouraging to read and apply them for this family setup to work. I believe the straitjacket moments are coming, but these scriptures are tools that my Savior has equipped me with to assist along the way. Even if I think my Savior isn't listening, the above scriptures are a fact that God is always listening.

Chapter 10
The Seconds Don't Tell the Season

Some time has passed since my household changed; we are still working on helping our family. We are still here; everyone is getting along well. Some of the challenges we thought we would face haven't been an issue at all. My granddad and dad get along well, my granddad is always on the go, and my dad is mobile in the first half of the day while he likes to watch TV in the second half of the day. Life is always a challenge regardless of who stays with you. But I'm glad they are good with one another. Not that I was expecting trouble, but I wasn't 100% sure. Their rooms are on opposite sides of the house, so they don't really cross paths.

Granddad lives a more refreshing life; he drives a luxury car, shares stories of his life, is more social, walks and shops around town. My dad, on the other hand, has Alzheimer's disease, so he has a caretaker with him when Tiffany and I are at work as we take care of him when we are home to keep the cost low.

So, he lives a different lifestyle than my granddad. Both are nice, respectful men, but one has a troubled disease while the other doesn't. This is one of the hard parts of going up. As a kid, I thought my dad was a superman or another superhero, and now in his later years, he has a disease that is taking away his superpowers. The part about life that isn't discussed much in households is when the parent and child roles are reversed. As I stated earlier, my dad didn't want to go back the home cause of this disease that is stealing his memories away from him. So why not be around family so, in his final memories, he will know he has around loved ones. People might read this and feel differently, which is okay, but I like to deal with facts and not false claims. There are people who will never help, no matter what. This is where I tend to lean more on my Savior instead of giving up and having a straitjacket moment.

Chapter 11
Confusion Grows

My father has just celebrated a milestone birthday, and my grandfather celebrated his about two weeks apart from one another. Both enjoyed their special days, one remembered the day, and for the other one, that day was kind of cloudy. Life has a unique way of making you just learn to appreciate each moment of each day you are still breathing. Nowadays, life presents a different challenge from what I expected, with ups and downs. Seeing my dad go through this is humbling because he is actually the one with the disease so, I can only imagine how it must feel to not remember simple things. This thing is trial and error; there is no manual or blueprint on how to deal with my dad. My dad is an alpha male who provided for his family from an early age and is still providing for his family to this day to a lesser degree now. He was raised in a Caribbean home. His parents migrated to the US from Jamaica, and he learned from a strict hand. So, he ruled with a somewhat iron fist, more like iron speech than a fist; whatever he said goes, and if he didn't say it, he doesn't believe it. As a child, until I left home as an adult, he used to tell me from time to time what good is knowledge if you don't share it? Nowadays, I wish I had asked him to explain that statement more and how he applied it to his life. I know now that his example was by living a good respectful life, being a person with integrity, and loving your family, even if it's from a distance. During this August, I wonder how much of our conversations he even remembers or how much the disease has destroyed the details of those memories. I regret that I didn't have more conversations about his view on parenthood and marriage. I can't stress enough to whoever reads this that if you have loved ones, ask questions about their past. Ask them, don't make the mistake of waiting. Cherish your time spent with them.

Alzheimer's disease is a disease I wish I could fight. I wish it was a person so I could find them and destroy it, so this relentless disease would never bother anyone again. Sadly, it's not; Alzheimer's is an unforgivable disease. It doesn't care how many people it will hurt or how many families it brings frustration too. It is undefeated, and there is no known cure for it. Medicine might slow it down but isn't 100% effective. Life is dangerous, diseases are dangerous, and this disease is on another level of danger.

According to alz.org,

Alzheimer's worsens over time. Alzheimer's is a progressive disease, where dementia symptoms gradually worsen over a number of years. In its early stages, memory loss is mild, but with late-stage Alzheimer's, individuals lose the ability to carry on a conversation and respond to their environment. Alzheimer's is the sixth-leading cause of death in the United States. Those with Alzheimer's live an average of eight years after their symptoms become noticeable to others, but survival can range from four to twenty years, depending on age and other health conditions. Moderate Alzheimer's disease (middle-stage)

During the moderate stage of Alzheimer's, individuals may have greater difficulty performing tasks such as paying bills, but they may still remember significant details about their life.

Moderate Alzheimer's is typically the longest stage and can last for many years. As the disease progresses, the person with Alzheimer's will require a greater level of care. You may notice the person with Alzheimer's confusing words, getting frustrated or angry, or acting in unexpected ways, such as refusing to bathe. Damage to nerve cells in the brain can make it difficult to express thoughts and perform routine tasks.

At this point, symptoms will be noticeable to others and may include:

-Forgetfulness of events or about one's own personal history

-Feeling moody or withdrawn, especially in socially or mentally challenging situations

-Being unable to recall their own address or telephone number or the high school or college from which they graduated

-Confusion about where they are or what day it is

-The need for help choosing proper clothing for the season or the occasion

-Trouble controlling bladder and bowels in some individuals

-Changes in sleep patterns, such as sleeping during the day and becoming restless at night

-An increased risk of wandering and becoming lost

-Personality and behavioral changes, including suspiciousness and delusions or compulsive, repetitive behavior like hand-wringing or tissue shredding

This is the stage that my father is at now and has been for close to three years. He has flashes of being great with certain topics while others he is somewhat lost with. Things he remembers are past childhood experiences or NYPD work stories that I heard about when I was a child. He remembers his birthday, SSN, address, certain other important information but can't remember my kids' names, whom he has known for over many years, or even remember what day of the week or year it is. His excuse for that is he is retired now. Why does the day of the week matter cause every day is Saturday for him, except going to church; he knows that happens on Sundays. But he recalls President Obama's name from time to time as he would refer to him as the only guy cooler than him. The schedule and routine are something we are strict with because we know that my dad is more stable when he follows a schedule. He is prior Military; prior NYPD whose stressed the importance of sticking to a schedule, so we have created a schedule for him because hopefully, the disease hasn't erased his ability to follow it. Some days, he is great with it, while other days, he is confused. The crazy thing about Alzheimer's disease is that my dad can be fine one minute, then one thing out of schedule can change most of his day and mood. It is one of the most unpredictable diseases. If my dad doesn't get the same spoon for breakfast, then his afternoon might be thrown off. He might get frustrated for no reason; there have been times that I have seen him smiling, talkative, and pleasant; later that day, he is quiet, confused, not sure of what he wants to say or do.

Every person that suffers from Alzheimer's disease is affected differently. Most start with memory loss and can live the rest of their lives with just some memory loss. While others can be destroyed mentally physically, and some forget to eat, so they starve to death. Alzheimer's disease is oftentimes called 'the long goodbye' because it can turn a perfectly normal person one day into a shell of their former self years later. A slow death, that's painful for them, I'm sure, but just as painful for family members. There are various reasons people have a difficult life, but seeing a person die mentally before the physical is no joke. Maybe losing my mom and Jamison was preparing Tiffany and me to deal with my father and his Alzheimer's disease.

My dad is now starting to roam, trying to go for walks outside by himself, which won't ever happen with us because I'm not sure if he can make it back to my home. We don't take chances with my dad and this unpredictable and menacing Alzheimer's disease. That's why everyone in this house helps out to the best of their abilities, and we have caretakers come in to assist as well.

Life is never fair; who knew the pain from losing my mom and Jamison was going to prepare me to take care of my dad?

Sometimes in life, people you don't know will help you more than people you do. Sometimes I would reach out to people for help, but I would hear from them that they were busy. In my mind, when I hear the term 'I'm busy,' I think, but you're really busy *doing what?* Video games, being lazy, collecting debt, being a hater, wasting time that could be someone's reality when they say they're busy. Respect me enough to tell me the truth, lying to me, but you're really lying to yourself. Don't play me for a fool just because you enjoy losing. SEE RIGHT THERE was a straitjacket moment that happens when you don't focus on the positive.

When people show you who they are, believe them, and if you don't like who they are, then run from them. Depending on how toxic they've been toward you, they might stay away because they know you don't want those negative vibes around you.

Complaining doesn't add value to your life; discipline adds value, working, faith, and prayer bring value. Helping others win should always be the motto.

Chapter 12

Deep Decline

I have skipped talking about some days because that time has been mostly the same. Some great times and some not so great, but overall if my dad stayed this way, he could live with us forever. Yes, do we get tired, but there are enough resources in the home and coming to the home makes things easier to deal with. No excuses were ever made to not help my dad, and as much as my dad has been there for people. I have noticed how many people aren't around for him. They have disappeared or tried to blame me for them not helping. The guilt in them is overflowing; you understand that people will blame everyone for their shortcomings but themselves. But I knew people wouldn't show up. I knew that before we were on weird terms. They barely showed up for my mom and continued to lie about it when asked. So, dad's situation wouldn't be any different.

Well, there's a saying that says, 'tomorrow never comes.' In life, people will make excuses and expect you to believe those trash excuses. Try not to focus on excuse-makers; focus on the people who call and visit. The people who visit allow my family and me to recharge and resume more refreshed. They also remind you that you are doing a good thing even though challenging it is good. People just remember no matter what good you are doing; there will be people out there hating—hating more than they ever helped. Don't stop helping because time will show that helping is always better than hating.

At this stage, life for my dad has tremendously declined. This Alzheimer's disease has progressed massively. Witnessing the brain dying before the body is heartbreaking. When you decide to take on helping a person with Alzheimer's, you are doing something that they at some point will dislike you for or not be able to remember the assistance you provided. I believe I have been through various experiences in my life that have helped in training me for dealing with this. From dealing with the loss of my mom and Jamison, being a foster parent, as well as growing up in a home where helping others was standard. Even if I think back far enough, my grandmother (my dad's mother) had this same disease, and I can never remember a time when she knew who I was.

Who knows what the future holds? I'm sure if my dad knew that Alzheimer's disease was in his future, he would have lived with more urgency. For most of his life, he was just working, providing for others, and paying bills. Now he is retired, but his money just goes to his bills. Paying for a memory care facility is the greatest bill now, more than any other bill he had in his life. The same goes for my mom. If she knew cancer would kill her, I'm sure she would have taken vacations or something. I just want everyone to know that I love my parents deeply; they provided for my siblings and me way more than I could have ever imagined. They were the best parents ever; I just wonder what if, sometimes. You must save for the future but also enjoy your present. Be in the moment. Go on walks with your loved ones, play board games, watch TV together, even if you can't take vacations because money is tight. Trust me, we all go through that, but free experiences can still be memorable ones.

Pain or grief is going to happen if you live long enough. Life doesn't wait for you to get to a certain age before you live it. Life is going to happen, and when disaster strikes, do you want to look back at your life with regret or boredom because you gave a job your life and didn't do anything but work, complain about the commute to and from, complain about the people, pay with credit cards, and don't have anything to look back on and be able to say you lived a full life. Listen, maybe people in society insist on just paying bills and dying; maybe I'm too concerned with seeing others as well as myself win. Their definition of winning might be totally opposite to mine. I'm not sure, but I know if I'm paying bills, it might as well be something memorable. I appreciate all my parents have done for me. I really do; I just want my life to be filled with great memories and be able to share with my children more. I want to take the baton from my parents, share loving memories and add new ones to my life and family's lives.

My parents going through these diseases have made me realize that you should create active memories (trips to the park, vacations, playing sports with your kids or loved ones, playing cards or board games) as well as save for your future. I want to leave my children with a legacy that will provide generational blessings.

Proverbs 13:22 A good person leaves an inheritance for their children's children.

Now, no matter what your beliefs are, everyone can agree that this makes sense. The reality is you can pass down riches, or you can pass down excuses to the generations to follow. Execution is rewarded, and excuses will ruin your opportunities to leave an inheritance. Listen, I don't have or want to seem like I have my entire life incomplete order, but I do understand the importance of doing so; I have been broke, busted, but battle-tested. So, I completely want everyone to achieve financial freedom early on.

With my dad's disease progressing, he's been moved to a memory care facility. This morning around 5:50 am, while I was driving to work, I got a phone call from a number I didn't recognize. I answered it with skepticism; it happened to be a medical technician from my dad's memory care facility, letting me know that my father is now being uncooperative, and they need my assistance. I had to go, but I couldn't believe they called me at this hour. I'm praying that everything is as good as it can be, but who knows? Once I got to the facility, my dad was sitting on the floor of another person's room. I got there, and he still recognized me, so he got off the floor and returned to his room, then lay down, saying he was tired and just needed some rest. I'm like, wow, if every visit was that easy. I wish this disease didn't exist; my dad was a strong alpha male who didn't want help. He was the one who always helped others. He only accepted help from people who had their own or people that cared. Helping him and meeting him where he is mental is a challenge the more this disease progresses.

MARCH is MADNESS for real. Dad went back to the ER for a UTI (urinary tract infection). It's crazy because UTIs mess with his mentality even more. He is way more confused, combative, and irritated than his normal baseline. I don't wish this disease on anyone; it breaks a person down to the point where there is no quality of life. Every day so far this month has been challenging for my dad and my family. This is the crazy thing about life; it doesn't wait for you to get all your ducks in a row before you choose to appreciate it. You must have life f***ed up if you think life is going to wait for you to have a perfect setup. Things will happen, and things will be challenging, so I tell people all the time to live their life while they're in the right mind and health. Prior to this disease, dad worked, had hobbies, and paid bills. Now even in his condition, he is using his income to pay bills, medical ones that cost way more than another bill combined he had previously. Some people have their opinions on how someone should be treated with Alzheimer's disease. Okay, can you come to visit, purchase these home remedies or even show me stories, websites, or rumors on these hood remedies reversing Alzheimer's disease or show how they slow down the disease? People say things sometimes just to hear themselves talk. Bless their hearts, people mean well but don't really mean what they say. Show up, and if you give tips, I can follow better in person or share information that is valid. Call doctors, medical professionals, or even holistic homies and ask them how your hood remedy works. Then share the exact process, not 'oh just try this, maybe try that.' They won't be there in person to help or even check up on the process but do it so they can say I told you. I never heard of anyone finding a cure for this disease. Not even the remedies (professional or non-professional) haven't had any success rate. This Alzheimer's disease/ dementia is UNDEFEATED; it destroys the individual and the family to an extent, the long goodbye. I totally understand why the long goodbye is another term for Alzheimer's disease. Some straitjacket moments have a lot of truth to them; you just can't stay in those moments for too long, though. Here are the stages:

https:// www.stellarliving.com/resources/memory-care/7-stages-dementia-explained/

What are the 7 stages of dementia? The 7 Stages of Dementia Explained

1. Dementia Stage One – Pre-illness.
2. Dementia Stage Two – Very mild signs of cognitive decline.
3. Dementia Stage Three – Signs of decline go from very mild to mild.
4. Dementia Stage Four – Moderate cognitive decline.
5. Dementia Stage Five – Moderately severe signs of cognitive decline.
6. Dementia Stage Six – Severe dementia.
7. Dementia Stage Seven -Extremely severe dementia loss of motor skills.

This Alzheimer's is a ratchet mess; my dad has now developed what the doctors call Psychotic Dementia. He is more aggressive and talks louder, like yelling and hollering at people. The sad part is he wasn't a psychotic person at all, not even in the most recent years of having Alzheimer's disease. This disease has changed my dad into a different person, he shows signs of being the great father he was prior to this disease, but those times are becoming less frequent.

Psychotic features of dementia include hallucinations (usually visual), delusions, and delusional misidentifications. Patients who display physical or verbal aggression, which often is associated with delusional misidentification, may require a combination of pharmacologic and non-pharmacologic treatments.

Feb 15, 2006 <u>Behavior Disorders of Dementia: Recognition and Treatment – AAFP</u>
https://www.aafp.org/afp/2006/0215/p647.html

"Psychosis may pose a greater challenge than cognitive decline for patients with dementia and their caregivers. The nature and frequency of psychotic symptoms varies over the course of illness, but in most patients, these symptoms occur more often in the later stages of disease. Management of psychosis requires a comprehensive nonpharmacologic and pharmacologic approach, including an accurate assessment of symptoms, awareness of the environment in which they occur, and identification of precipitants and how they affect patients and their caregivers. Nonpharmacologic interventions include counseling the caregiver about the nonintentional nature of the psychotic features and offering coping strategies. Approaches for the patient involve behavior modification; appropriate use of sensory intervention, environmental safety, and maintenance of routines such as providing meals, exercise, and sleep on a consistent basis.

Pharmacologic treatments should be governed by a "start low, go slow" philosophy; a mono sequential approach is recommended, in which a single agent is titrated until the targeted behavior is reduced, side effects become intolerable, or the maximal dosage is achieved. Atypical antipsychotics have the greatest effectiveness and are best tolerated. Second-line medications include typical antipsychotics for short-term therapy; and, less often, anticonvulsants, acetylcholinesterase inhibitors, antidepressants, and anxiolytics. Goals of treatment should include symptom reduction and preservation of quality of life."

This disease can make the smartest strongest, or even nicest person change into someone extremely different. Alzheimer's is called the long goodbye for a reason; watching a loved one go from full of life to lifeless is tragic. The role from parent to child changes as they need the help they provide to us. Many stories can be told about how parents or relatives were once very productive in life but could not talk, walk, or even chew food because of this disease.

My dad was an extremely smart man. He was college-educated, graduated Magna Cum Laude, retired US Military, retired law enforcement after having a long and distinguished career. But most of all, he was a great family man. His memories are being destroyed with each blink of an eye by this disease. So many families have had their plans altered; the loved one who has this disease didn't expect this disease to happen to them. They worked or lived their whole life, possibly waiting for retirement to live. Work forty years then retire, by then anyone would hope to have some serious savings or a pension to enjoy their retirement with, but then BOOM, they start forgetting the little things until they become major. Then other loved ones have to assist them in their daily functions if the loved ones are in a position to. Some folks don't have anyone that can help them out. They go into facilities to spend the rest of their lives rotting away. Most people don't plan for the future. Some put life on hold until retirement or even wait until they get all of their ducks in a row to enjoy life. But life doesn't work that way, especially with Alzheimer's disease; this disease will sneak up on a person and choke them out. Leaving them possibly mindless hopeless, and if they have supportive families, it will do the same thing or worse. Everyone who has this terrible disease is affected by it differently. But the same result happens to all of them, death. There are so many days that I sit back and wonder when did this disease get a hold on my dad? Was it always around but just dormant? Was it him being in a war, stress from being a police officer and parent, or the food he ate? Who knows? Did my dad exhibit signs early? I wonder at times why God chose my family to experience this. I am fully aware that everyone faces some challenges that they wouldn't wish on their worst enemy, but come on, God, this disease is so unforgiving. At times, he can't even remember his name, nor can he remember to give thanks to you, God.

The thing about life that I'm trying to say to many of us is to work on not getting so busy that you forget to live life. So many of us are focused on going to work and giving our loved ones our leftover time. We know leftovers don't taste as good with food, so why do we do it with life? We go through life just living to pay bills, but what experiences will you have to show for it? Sneakers get old, vacations you cherish, clothes get faded, spending quality time with family and friends means more than being stuck in traffic complaining about things you can't control. A productive person is aware of how they are spending their time, and they have goals, so they are using the time they have to be productive. In this reflection of my life, I totally understand when I act like a child, I become busy, just moving without purpose. Everyone can make smarter decisions if they can learn from obstacles. Setbacks will happen, but don't get too down; if you live long enough, you will be sad or disappointed in people or in the fact that they pass away. Work hard, smile, and try to have some fun. Pray for a sane mind and body because once your mind goes before your body, that's a living nightmare for you and your family if they want to be around you during those dark times.

My dad was the most serious person I met in my life. He was very strict and used to tell me, since I have two older siblings, that if I didn't learn from their mistakes, then my punishments would be the worst. So, I paid attention as my life depended on it, and in some cases, it probably did. He was also extremely book smart, I think he told me he read over 5,000 books, and I asked him why? He told me because he never wanted anyone to get over him, nor did he ever want to be unprepared for life when he got older. I was around fifteen when he told me that, and I was like, man, I just want to play basketball and talk to girls, not read books.

But at the time, I didn't realize he was trying to drop some game on me. This disease that my dad has makes me reminisce on the many conversations we had at various times in my life. Almost like he was trying to prepare me for what I'm dealing with now. We talked more as I got older, like in my college years, and more once I prepared to move out of his home to become my own man. I think it is extremely important to leave the nest when you are mentally ready, be financially ready as well but also understand that once you leave, you should only come back to visit. Just my opinion, God's plan is different for everyone, and some people are way more ahead of me in life, and they came back to the nest, so I just think that leaving the nest was the best thing for me and my situation. Dad was the biggest factor in my leaving home, almost like God told him that he needed me to leave when I did. We would spend hours talking about the journey I was going to embark on. He would share his stories of leaving home for the military and how he thanked God every day that he left cause when he would come back to visit, too many friends and neighbors weren't doing that well or just had no plan on how to advance in life. I left right after college and often came back to visit; heck by me, moving gave my parents more of a reason to travel. Now they could come to see me and teach me more about being an adult since I could relate more to their adult jokes or the 'having your own place' stories they shared with me. Every time I would visit, or when they came to visit, they would buy me home goods and give me money for gas or something.

They would always tell me to accept the help, don't take it as a sign of offense, even if you don't need it, because as parents, they felt like I was paying attention to how they tried to help me develop into a man. My parents would always tell me once you have kids of your own, it will make way more sense then.

My dad has been in a nursing home for the past several months, and now there are hidden fees that have come up; the facility charges monthly to clean his private areas, plus charging him for a diaper rash prevention cream and a host of other things. He doesn't even remember his own name most of the time, unable to walk and talk with comprehensive conversations. At times I believe life has given him the middle finger and left him in the rearview just to suffer and die. Praying for things to get better doesn't happen on my time or anyone else.

I pray that anyone who is experiencing a possible straitjacket moment doesn't go the straitjacket route but finds a Savior to help put them onto a better route.

Chapter 13

Punched in the Face Just for Living

There are so many events that have occurred in my life that I had to write this book. I needed a release valve or just a platform where I could vent. I wanted to share with people that no matter the pain, please don't give up. We all have obstacles in our lives that produce those Savior vs. Straitjacket moments. Whether it's the loss of a loved one, a regret, first heartbreak, prison sentence, or something so challenging that makes you realize you have come to a fork in the road and you must choose a path. Some events force you to choose a path, and there is no time to debate; immediate action must happen, and depending on the decision, it might be your Savior vs. straitjacket moment. Sometimes in life, you have to face challenges that will surprise the s*** out of you but stand tall and find the strength to dig deep and get help to make it through. How you deal with grief is going to depend on how you find your Savior over the straitjacket.

Seeing my dad break down because of a disease was just a mess. What did he do in life to deserve this? He is also unable to speak clearly anymore. We are not sure if it's from the disease or the medication he is on. I don't wish Alzheimer's disease on my worst enemy. To see someone's brain die before their body is like a punch in the face. But I have dealt with sadness before, and I understand God doesn't make mistakes. I appreciate that God allowed me to have so many positive and meaningful moments with my loved ones while they went through their last days. Everyone processes grief differently.

Chapter 14
Still Gets Dark at Times

Random times, even after all these years, I am faced with mentally confusing times. I just want to become sad and complain because I try to envision what life would be like if Jamison and mom were still physically here as well as my dad mentally still being sharp. Those moments sometimes take a weird toll on my mind and spirit. My dad celebrated his seventy-eighth birthday a few weeks ago. Seeing him in the state that he is in is difficult to watch. He had some other family come to see him, and the whole time we were with him, he was sleeping. A few times, he would open his eyes and smile, but you could tell he wasn't there anymore. His mind is gone, but he's physically there. Alzheimer's disease doesn't allow anyone to get their ducks in a row before it strikes heavy. Seeing my dad go through this makes me want to live my life with more urgency than ever before. Some days I want to rest, but then I think if I rest now, I might regret it later. Too many people need or even want help or just someone else to relate to.

I wrote this book to remind people that they're not alone in this world. Yes, none of us walk around with name tags or stamps on our heads that tell others what we are dealing with but conversing with others in a respectful way can be extremely helpful. You can't tell everyone your business, but some people can know just enough to hold a conversation. The disease didn't even allow my dad to appreciate his own birthday; he sometimes smiled when he was awake, and someone said Happy Birthday to him, but he didn't say anything. The whole time some of my family and I were at the nursing home my dad was at; he was just sleeping in his reclining chair. There were times that no matter how much we tried to wake him up and keep him awake, he would just go back to sleep, but when it was time to eat his lunch, he woke up for that and ate all his food. Afterward, he went right back to sleep again. My dad speaks very little now, and most of the time, it doesn't refer to anything but his prior career as a police officer. How sad is it that on your own birthday, you can't even realize that it is your own actual birthday? A reminder that this Alzheimer's disease is nothing to play with, no cures, no treatment to reverse the condition, nothing.

Chapter 15
Fade Away

I gave my dad a haircut while he was sleeping; it was a different kind of feeling I had. Different meaning, I thought it was cool to do, but given the circumstances, it sucked. My dad was never really the haircut type of person, even though he looked better when he had one versus not having a haircut. For as long as I can remember, my dad always had the convertible top with the tinted windows up for a hairstyle. For the readers that don't know what I mean, look up a picture of George Jefferson from the TV sitcom, The Jeffersons. Growing up and seeing my dad with a lot of hair never really bothered me. I knew that I could never do that. Everyone is different when it comes to haircuts, and that's cool.

This disease that my dad is suffering from makes me reminisce on my childhood and how the things I experienced and relationships I developed came about. My parents did a great job raising my siblings and me. I wonder if I paid enough attention. My parents were amazing and did the best they could. Maybe they were dealing with having three children with three different personalities along with their own. So maybe my dad wanted to get more haircuts but just didn't want to sit in a barbershop and wait, or maybe he didn't care about a haircut. I just know, either way, I was paying attention to those small things even as a child. Sometimes life and work get in the way of living; pay attention to life people because neither of my parents expected to have grandkids that they never met or don't remember meeting. Maybe, me taking care of my dad is God's way of saying make sure you are active in your kids' lives. I think back to the many things my dad decided to teach me when I was a shorty. He taught me how to ride a bike, how to study, how to change a flat tire, and many more. I just try to think about those things when I spend time with him.

Chapter 16

Mumble Rap

My dad's speech has diminished so much to the point that if he even speaks, 75% of that time, he is mumbling. I have to be very quiet when he talks, and most of the prolonged speech doesn't make much sense. This Alzheimer's disease is a nasty and vile disease. It doesn't care who you are, how you treat people, nothing. It brings a person and their family down and places weird energy around them. I talked to my dad, just hoping he still understands me but also hoping he would say, hey Chris, stop talking and let me get a word or two in, please. I pray that my Savior has kept my dad from his own Straitjacket moments. My dad's various actions attitude while having this Alzheimer's Disease might have been his straitjacket moments, but God kept him from being able to remember them.

Surviving is exactly what my dad is doing, which at this stage is mind-blowing. He doesn't talk much or even open his eyes, but his appetite is still strong.

He hasn't walked at all in over eight months. So just imagine if your feet haven't hit the pavement in over eight months and physically you were able to, but your mind is so destroyed that the brain can't tell your body to move, let alone walk. I can't believe the strength my dad has shown during this process; it must be the strength to be able to continue going on even when your mind is already checked out. I hope people are reading this understand the importance of living and enjoying life while you are in the right state of mind.

Chapter 17
Getting Out of the Funk

Besides praying for a higher power to assist and deliver me from the low points in my life, I decided to strengthen my mind and body. (Except I still have a sweet tooth.) The mental thing I started doing is focusing on the positive things that go on daily. I have several things I say on a daily basis:

- Attack the day with positive vibes
- Help others win
- Talk to God in a respectful way
- Think about better times
- Appreciate the great memories
- Don't dwell on the past; make a short revisit

Attack the day with positive vibes is a challenging one because there are days that I mentally don't want to be positive. But I have found out from being in my darkest moment that you need light to effectively navigate through the darkness. You have to find the bright spots in each day, thanking God for breath, being able to open your eyes and see another day, because when I was processing the loss of my mom and Jamison, I didn't see positively immediately. But going through the storm of losing them allowed me to assist my dad in his troubling time with the deadly disease called Alzheimer's. Find a bright spot every day.

Helping others win is something to try to enforce in your life. Don't hate on anyone; try to assist people if you can. If they win, that's a great thing. Never be jealous or envious of anyone because if they shine, then you shine as well. One hand washes, the other is an old term I'm sure all of us have heard at one point or another. There is no time to hate; there's only time to help. I hope people reread this if they find themselves hating on anyone, especially if that person is doing legal things to win.

Talking to God is challenging when things aren't going my way. I don't have a problem praising him when I'm being blessed. My mom used to tell me when I was a kid that she is my parent, not my friend, and neither is God. She would say that God and she can be friendly but never my friends. God is in the ultimate position to help, but that doesn't mean God has to be your friend. When I got in trouble, she would say, "You like sports, right?" I would say, "Yes, mom." "You know the owner and coach of the Yankees, right?" I'd say, "Yes, mom." Well, she should say think of God as the owner of your life and your parents as the managers, and we have to put you on a path for you to succeed. If you don't follow us, then life will be harder than you could ever imagine. In the back of my mind, I was joking, saying, well, managers get fired all the time like the Yankees fire them. But I never had enough courage or stupidity to say that to her and especially not God.

Thinking about better times can make you the most emotional because depending on what the memory is, that could cause me to become sadder. But I would try to think about how my loved ones would want me to continue with life. Better times can be pleasant as well; after the initial sadness, I tend to get refocused on determining how impactful I want to be.

Don't dwell in the past. Make a short revisit there because if you don't, you will continue to think with that fractured mindset. This was a hard place; I was stuck too many times where I was, vacationing in the past. To the point, life was passing me by. I didn't want to stay there too long. Holding on to the past can cause greater problems in your future. I will share some more things that I thought of or learned about that helped in the past but still help me today.

Here are five ways how to go toward your Savior instead of straitjacket (how to get out of the funk) (what can work for anyone).

1. Prayer countless times
2. Therapy
3. Positive thoughts and actions
4. Getting away from negative energy
5. Drink water

Three things I learned from mom, dad, and Jamison

Mom:

- Show love to people
- Trust in God
- Be respectful

Dad:

- Be stern
- No gray area
- Respect authority

Jamison:

- Smile more
- Enjoy your time with others
- Take pictures

Chapter 18
Final Days

I have seen my dad slowly but surely lose simple things with each visit. Mind you, I visit him two to three times each week, and someone in my household visits four to five times. At this stage, we are all extremely active in my dad's life, especially since he has been in this facility. We have noticed from our own observations and hearing from the workers at the facility that it's rare that a family visits their loved one as often as my household. I told the workers that my dad was present in my life, so this was the least I could do. Seeing a loved one break down every day little by little doesn't make sense to me sometimes. My dad's ability to walk was one of the first things to go. He stopped walking, which prior to that, he was very mobile. It's crazy how the disease made him forget he was healthy enough to walk. He was still able to talk, but most of the time, he'd just talk about going to work and what he saw at work. He would speak to people when they would enter his room, but he would tend to go back to his own thoughts about work.

If you asked questions, he would answer and sometimes ask questions, so even though he wasn't walking, he would hold a conversation to an extent. So, in about eight months-time, he is unable to walk, talk and open his eyes constantly.

Alzheimer's disease has broken this superman down to where he doesn't even remember who he is anymore. Even while I'm writing this, emotions go through my mind because I think about how present my dad was in my life. But this also makes me realize that life doesn't wait for anyone to get all their so-called ducks in a row before you start living. I just wish God would have allowed my parents and Jamison to see and interact with everyone else. How come Jamison couldn't play and interact with his other siblings? I wonder these things all the time, but I respect my Savior, and perhaps life for my family would have been completely different if things didn't happen according to God's plan.

Chapter 19

No More Pain

MY DAD died today. I was at work when I got the message. In the days leading up to his transition, I saw his body break down at a faster rate than ever before. Severe weight loss, not speaking, not opening his eyes. So, many more things were happening that gave warning, but the emotions hit differently when he passed. I got to work early that morning just to finish up some things, and my wife called me around 6:25 am to tell me dad passed. I worked about ten minutes from his facility, so I drove as swift and safely as possible but with a clear understanding that he was no longer suffering. No matter my selfish emotions that I wanted him to continue to live, I realized that God needed him more. I love my dad deeply, and with no regrets, I was able to see him before he passed—the first family member to see him after he passed. I don't say that to show any badge of honor but just to say that another process has started, and I have to be present in helping dad.

I called on my Lord and Savior to just give me understanding, patience, peace, and a clear mind on how to handle making the required arrangements to have a proper burial for my dad. I do have help, but this is the time to activate the help button and grieve button to get things done with excellence. I cried as I prayed, standing by my dad's bedside once I got to the facility. His physical body was still in his room, with the room as coldest as possible to ensure his body stayed good enough to be transported. When I got to his room, a white sheet was over his entire body, just like in the movies. I pulled the sheet back and saw my dad no longer suffering from this deadly Alzheimer's disease.

I know my dad is with my mom and Jamison, in a better place and hugging them like never before. I envision dad, mom, and Jamison all together talking, laughing, and smiling. Jamison and my mom showing my dad around heaven and introducing him to the wonderful people and God. Even writing this brings out the emotions I have. To whoever reads this book, when you experience the loss of an active parent, it hits different. I haven't been to work the last few days, and no one expects me to come in yet, especially prior to his burial. I need this time off to reflect on three great lives that have made a generational impact on my life, and if I come close to that, I am beyond blessed. Even though my dad just passed, the emotions from losing my mom and Jamison hit me as well. The emotion is nowhere as intense as years ago but still intense. I pray my Savior will not only help me with processing this loss but my family as well. Some people deal with grief differently, and I have been praying for patience, peace, and understanding. The following is the speech I want to say at my dad's funeral as I write this, it is subject to change:

My family and I would like to thank everyone for showing their love during this difficult time with the loss of dad. He was a great man to people and especially was an amazing father to his children. He wanted his children to do great in their own paths, and I can say, dad, you got what you wanted. We are all successful in life because of the active presence you had in ours. You and mom set the bar, and we appreciate you both for that. Dad, we will forever miss you but know you are with mom, and she is taking you on tour around

Heaven. You were perfect for us. You showed us when to be serious and stern with people while being fun to be around. Even in your verbal and non-verbal communications, you left a lasting impact. I can't thank you enough, no matter what we went through in life, you were there, and we did our best to return the favor. You've impacted so many people's lives in a way that will live longer than any of us. God continues to be with us going forward. God bless and thank you, everyone.

I pray that I will be able to get through this process smoothly with no hiccups. My savior is undefeated when it comes to assisting me with my issues, and I pray this will be no different. I know that funerals can be very emotional, and I must respect the fact that everyone grieves differently. When certain emotions go up, intelligence goes down, so I must be mindful of my tone, facial expressions, and other things.

My dad's funeral was kind of a whirlwind full of emotions for myself and others. I didn't cry, but many times I felt like I was, while anger, sadness, happiness were more present than anything else. I just spoke to people almost detached from emotions. Not only is my dad gone, but both my parents are no longer here in the physical form, which most people might not understand how difficult that is, whether your parents are active in your life or deadbeats, at least you know one or both are alive. In my case, I can't say that. I can't go to them and get new advice; now, I just think back on the memories and conversations of old to help me in times of need. That's the most difficult part about seeing loved ones pass away; you can't have new conversations with them anymore. You can only revisit memories in your mind. The tricky part is when regret sets in. All the time while I was younger, I could/should have paid more attention or had longer conversations. I know my parents would never want me to regret anything because they have seen me get married and start a family. In my dad's case, he saw me purchase a home that he would eventually live in. I can't imagine how my life would have been had my parents not had an active presence in my life. But I do know that because of them being active, I am more equipped to handle my future with them and God watching with delight going forward. I tell people from time to time that asks me how I am handling things now; I tell them I'm great because I have my folks in Heaven bragging about me, saying that's my boy down there. Mom and dad, you raised me well, I didn't always listen to everything, but the tools that are in my toolbox are well equipped to assist my family and me going forward. Job well done, mom, dad, and Jamison. In their lifetime, I know my parents looked out for my siblings and me. My family and I can never thank them enough. Back to my dad's funeral, there were about a hundred or so people that I had never heard about, some I hadn't seen in decades, some that were active in his life even when dealing with this deadly disease. I appreciate them all taking time out of their busy schedules to show their support and also to the people that couldn't make it that sent their condolences. The fact that my family tends to use funerals as family reunions are very disappointing. Perhaps, I need to host or organize family functions. I can't fault anyone but myself because I could host family events or break the cycle and start a family gathering or something of that nature. Back to my dad's funeral, there were many people who shared memories that they experienced with my dad. Some I didn't know, and others I have heard. Overall everyone spoke extremely highly of my dad, and I have to live the rest of my life carrying that torch. My last name is bigger than me; the men who share the last name that came before me are men that were respected, respectful, honorable, and didn't do gray areas when interacting with others. I hope that I can raise my sons with the same understanding that your last name is one of honor and respect. Funerals make me realize that God is real and that life is precious and shouldn't be taken for granted.

The funeral also made me realize that I need to make a bigger impact on my family; I pray that no one gets Alzheimer's disease. Being that my dad was a former NYPD and US Army, his funeral service was done with honor. At the funeral, there were NYPD and US Army, there making sure everything was done with ease. The NYPD's honor guard was there to carry my dad's casket; we got a police escort to his burial site as well as being presented with an American flag by the military.

The loved ones that I lost in the last several years have meant so much to me and everyone that knew them; their legacy will live on forever. My dad lived an amazing life. I cannot lie; there are most likely things I don't know, but for the things I do know, it's safe to say my dad was dope. He loved his family, a great deal more than we might ever realize. My mom was an incredible woman who represented excellence. She was one of the few people I have ever met that could be among good, bad, and weird people, and they all would say, 'Yo your moms is mad cool.' She met people where they were, not judging people, just understanding people are all different. My son Jamison smiled every day, which is something I never did prior to him being born. Their positive traits live on in me as I try my best to represent them to the best of my abilities. I make mistakes that probably make them shake their heads in heaven but more often than not, I believe I make them proud.

It's the first Christmas in my life that none of my parents are with us. Christmas was my parents' favorite time of the year. Even though the last few Christmases haven't been the best for my dad, at least he was still alive for them. The hardest thing for me about not having either parent around is just seeing the joy and happiness that they showed. Also, the memories of how my family and I have applied some of the Christmas traditions I learned from my parents. Now I just have memories of my parents around Christmas time going forward. Hopefully, they are in a greater place, experiencing no pain or memory loss, or any negative issues. The holidays are the times when neither parent being alive is the most emotional for me because I learned from them about the importance of family time. I must do a better job of sharing those holidays with my family so that they can have a loving experience the same way I did with my parents. The things we face we could either make excuses on or execute. My dad would also say if getting mad will solve your problem, then get mad, but if it won't, then use that energy for something better. Often, we focus on the problem, and not enough energy goes into finding a positive solution.

Jamison and my dad

Chapter 20

Conclusion: Fear vs. Fact

Below is a part of something I wrote and shared with my church a few summers ago for Father's Day. This is somewhat a summary of this book but was one of the main reasons I needed to write and complete this book.

"Before I go, I want to leave you with a defining moment in my life; back on Christmas Eve, I got married to my better half. A short time after, we were blessed to have a son named Jamison; at that time, he was the only child I knew about. He was my mother's first grandchild; he smiled every day no matter what. No matter how my day went, I knew when I got home from work that I'd see his smile, and he smiled often. Fast forward to July 4th, my mother was called home to be with the Lord (passed away), then my son Jamison was called home to be with the Lord (passed away). I understood a child should bury a parent because EVEN though it HURTS, parents passing before their children is normally a natural process. It still hurts, though, BUT a parent shouldn't have to bury a child, especially a BABY, two devasting blows that still hurt to this day. HOW do I find MEANING in THAT? Jamison was only ten months and twenty-three days old and didn't get a chance to live a full life. I answer to a higher power, so even in my dark moments, I knew I had to find out WHY I'm here. Many of us are going through something, and you're focusing on the problem more than the solution. Stop empowering the

problem, the anger, and the grief. Instead, use that energy to awaken your calling. As a father, you sometimes must CRY your way through the difficult and most challenging of times, but you cannot GIVE UP. You cannot let the sadness sink you to a suffering space forever."

Even though my dad didn't pass away around the same time as my mom and Jamison, his loss still made me question if my Savior was still going to help. Seeing my dad battle Alzheimer's disease at times made me wonder if this was how my life would have been if I had chosen a straitjacket mindset or a facility that required one. There were times that I prayed for God to just give my dad's memories back to him and take mine from me. Why couldn't my parents and Jamison just die from old age or natural causes? The type of illnesses that makes me even want to question my own faith.

I pray that everyone can find a place in their hearts to love everyone, even if it's from a distance. Remember that time is precious, and nothing is guaranteed except death. No one knows when their time on this earth is over or how it will end. Take a moment to ask for forgiveness from God and pray that for however long you are alive, be sure to do something great with your time. Live with intention. Don't waste time being lazy, mean, and any other negative things; use that negative energy and focus on positive things. Don't be afraid to apologize to someone even if the issue isn't your fault, especially if you were on the best of terms prior to any disagreements. I know that it's easier said than done but make a genuine attempt and if the other party still doesn't accept your apology or change their behavior, then love them from a distance. PRAY for them, don't prey on them or try to recruit others to prey on them either.

Communication is an underlined KEY in not losing yourself. Fear the importance of learning, knowing, and defeating fear. The crazy part about my life as an adult is it has been filled with positive and negative things that I would have never imagined. I didn't plan for dealing with loss or plan for helping others win while I was going through my own storm. I tried to pay attention to elders or other people that made sense when they spoke to me. I firmly believe not everyone comes into your life to help; they come to disrupt your path. Some claim to be loyal to you, but they are only loyal to your unhappiness. I had to move differently to realize that stuff. Listen, everyone will face something at some point in their lives that will make them question everything and everyone, but I believe God gives you people, signs, and situations to help you lean closer to God to get through the troubles. You can make it through; you have to stay in the game of life long enough to see your blessings come true. I am a living testimony that if I can go through this draining process and come out living with my mind and body intact, then you can as well. Each day will present a new challenge, but you can make it through. I believe in you more than you know.

Most importantly, please seek help instead of trying to battle depression, grief, sadness, or any other straitjacket moments alone. Seek professional help. Seek help from peers, loved ones, spiritual advisors, don't be afraid to reach out. You can get past the grief and pain. You are an amazing person to the world. We must carry on the tradition of being good people. Your loved ones didn't leave just to leave you lost.

Please find your Savior Over Straitjacket.

Tiffany and I

Connect with Chris:

www.christophergranville.com

info@christophergranville.com

Instagram

christophergranvilleauthor

Facebook

ChristopherGranvilleAuthor

Made in the USA
Coppell, TX
21 April 2022

76846211R10059